Shocking
Sharks

by Gary Lopez

sundance™

A Haights Cross Communications Company

® sundance™
A Haights Cross Communications ™ Company

Sundance/Newbridge Educational Publishing, LLC
One Beeman Road
P.O. Box 740
Northborough, MA 01532-0740
800-343-8204
www.sundancepub.com

Adapted from *Naturebooks*, published in 2001 by The Child's World®, Inc.
P.O. Box 326
Chanhassen, MN 55317-0326

Photo Credits: Front cover © Stephen Frink, The Image Bank/Getty
Images; p. 2 © Eiichi Kurasawa, The National Audubon Society Collection/
Photo Researchers; p. 9 © Brandon D. Cole; pp. 13, 14, 21, 22 (top), 25
© Jeffrey L. Rotman; p. 17 © Marilyn Kazmers/Dembinsky Photo Assoc.,
Inc.; p. 18 © Rudolf Ingo Riepl/Animals Animals; p. 22 (bottom) © Leonard
L. T. Rhodes/Animals Animals; p. 26 © Fred McConnaughey, The National
Audubon Society Collection/Photo Researchers; p. 29 © Marilyn and Maris
Kazmers/Sharksong; p. 30 © Michele Westmorland/Animals Animals;
back cover, pp. 6, 10 © Tom Campbell/Art Womack Photography

ISBN-13: 978-0-7608-9347-0
ISBN-10: 0-7608-9347-0

Printed in China

Contents

Bright sun is shining down on the ocean. The water is clear and blue. Under the surface, schools of fish are swimming. But another animal cruises along with them. It has a long, sleek body and very sharp teeth. It is looking for something to eat. People all over the world **fear** this animal.

It's a **shark!**

This shark is swimming slowly as it searches for food.

2 What Do Sharks Look Like?

Sharks are part of the same animal family as fish. They have a long, round body and a **powerful tail.** Sharks have **fins** on the sides and top of their body. Their fins help them change direction as they swim. Sharks also have **thin slits** on the sides of their head. These **gills** are used for breathing.

A shark's skin is very rough. People say it feels **like sandpaper.** But it is really made up of tiny **scales.** The scales look a lot like the ones on a snake.

Here you can see the scales that make up a shark's skin.

This enormous shark eats the same food (plankton) as these small yellow fish!

Most sharks have dozens of **sharp teeth.** Their teeth help them hold on to slippery food. If a tooth **breaks** or falls out, another one grows in its place.

Not all sharks have teeth, though. Some have mouths that are lined with **small filters.** These sharks catch their food by opening up their **mouths** as they swim. Tiny animals called **plankton** get washed in. Then the filters trap the plankton for the sharks to eat.

Mmmm . . . plankton, my favorite!

There are **hundreds** of different kinds of sharks in the world. They each have their own special shape, size, and color. Some have spots. Some have **stripes.** Some are known for how big they are. The whale shark can be over 45 feet long! But the spined pygmy shark is much smaller than that. It grows to be only about 10 inches long.

This large tiger shark has stripes along the sides of its body.

4 ▶ Are Sharks Dangerous?

Small sharks are **fairly gentle** animals. Even many large sharks are harmless. But some can be very **dangerous.** The great white is one shark that should be left alone.

The **great white shark** can grow over 20 feet long. It may weigh almost 3,000 pounds! This shark hunts seals, sea lions, and dolphins. It kills these big animals with its strong jaws and **thousands** of teeth!

This huge great white shark is swimming near Australia's Dangerous Reef.

Sharks sometimes get very hungry, bothered, or even scared. This is when they are the most dangerous! They **might attack** a person when they feel this way.

Usually, sharks stay far away from people. They **don't really hunt people** like they do in the movies. But a shark can mistake a person for its usual food.

This shark is quickly turning away from something that frightened it.

5 How Do Sharks Hunt?

Sharks use all of their senses to find food. They can smell an animal from far away. They might see their prey as it swims by. They can also feel movements in the water around them. This tells sharks right where their prey is. When they get near an animal, sharks can also taste its "flavor" in the water.

This shark is eating a large fish called a grouper.

Small sharks have a different way of catching food than big sharks do. Small sharks slowly sneak up behind their prey. Then they quickly gulp down the animal!

Big sharks must work a little harder. They circle around their prey, trying not to scare it. When the shark is close enough, it dives under the animal. Then the shark quickly attacks. It bites down with its sharp teeth and eats the animal!

A great white shark is attacking some bait that was thrown into the water.

6 What Are Baby Sharks Like?

Most sharks give birth to their babies, or **pups.** The pups can swim as soon as they are born. Other sharks lay eggs. The eggs stick to rocks or weeds until they hatch. Like most animals, the babies look like small adults.

Mother sharks don't stay around to take care of their pups. The pups must learn to eat and stay safe all on their own.

Top Photo: This newly hatched shark still has its yolk sac connected to it.

Bottom Photo: This shark egg has washed up on a beach.

Sharks are very important animals. They help **keep the oceans healthy.** They do this by eating animals that are weak and sick. This gives the healthy animals more space to live in. Without **predators** such as sharks, the oceans would have too many animals. And many of them would be sick.

I hope those teeth don't get too close to me!

This shark is swimming at night off the coast of North Carolina.

8 Do Sharks Have Enemies?

Sharks don't have many enemies in the ocean. In fact, their biggest enemy is **people.** Some people who fish for a living might kill sharks. They don't want sharks to eat the fish they are trying to catch. Other people kill sharks just to sell their meat and fins. Sharks also die from getting caught in fishing nets by mistake.

This hammerhead shark died after getting caught in a net.

There is still a lot we do not know about sharks. Some kinds of sharks swim in very deep water. So we **know very little** about how they live. Scientists still have questions about sharks they see all the time! But they try to learn the answers by watching sharks in zoos. They also learn more by swimming with sharks. Scientists wear lots of **special equipment** to stay safe, of course!

A scientist is examining a lemon shark in the Bahamas.

28

Sharks are some of the most interesting animals in the world. Most people are **afraid** of them, though. They do not want to learn more about these animals.

But you may want to find out a lot more about sharks. Don't worry. There are still plenty of questions to be answered!

I am a great mystery waiting to be solved!

This great white shark is swimming just under the surface of the water.

Glossary

fins flaps on a fish's body that help it change direction while swimming

gills thin slits on a fish's body that are used for breathing; air from water gets trapped in them and enters the body of the animal

plankton tiny animals that some sea creatures eat

predators animals that hunt and kill other animals for food

pups baby sharks

scales small, hard plates that cover the skin of some animals